Girl-Boss

In a man's world

This is a first publication 2024

Copyright © 2024 Bianchina Publishing House

All rights reserved. No part of this publication may be reproduced or copied.

ISBN: 9798325071133

Chapter 1:   **PG 8**

Introduction

Navigating Male-Dominated Industries

Embracing Your Role as a Girl-Boss

Chapter 2:   **PG 10**

Challenging Gender Stereotypes

Recognizing and Overcoming Bias and Discrimination

Reframing Perceptions of Women in Leadership

Chapter 3:   **PG 19**

Cultivating Confidence and Assertiveness

Owning Your Voice and Value

Assertive Communication Strategies for Success

Chapter 4: PG 28
Building a Supportive Network

Finding Mentorship and Sponsorship Opportunities

Creating a Community of Empowered Women

Chapter 5: PG 38
Embracing Your Unique Strengths

Leveraging Female Leadership Traits

Finding Your Leadership Style and Voice

Chapter 6: PG 47
Overcoming Imposter Syndrome

Recognizing and Overcoming Self-Doubt

Celebrating Your Achievements and Abilities

Chapter 7:   **PG 56**

Negotiating Like a Pro

Strategies for Successful Salary Negotiations

Assertive Negotiation Techniques for Career Advancement

Chapter 8:   **PG 66**

Balancing Ambition with Self-Care

Prioritizing Work-Life Balance

Setting Boundaries and Practicing Self-Compassion

Chapter 9:   **PG 76**

Leading with Empathy and Compassion

Building Stronger Teams Through Emotional Intelligence

Creating Inclusive and Supportive Work Environments

Chapter 10: **PG 87**

Thriving in Leadership Roles

Overcoming Challenges as a Female Leader

Harnessing Your Leadership Potential for Positive Impact

Chapter 11: **PG 97**

Advocating for Gender Equality

Taking Action to Promote Diversity and Inclusion

Supporting Other Women in Their Career Journeys

Chapter 12:   **PG 108**

Breaking Barriers and Shattering Glass Ceilings

Paving the Way for Future Generations of Female Leaders

Leaving Your Mark on the World as a Girl-Boss

Chapter 13:   **PG 118**

Conclusion

Embracing Your Power and Potential as a Girl-Boss

Committing to Continued Growth and Leadership

Chapter 14:   **PG 128**

Additional Resources

Books, Podcasts, and Websites on Women in Leadership

Organizations and Networks for Female Professionals

Disclaimer: The information provided in this Book is for educational and informational purposes only and is not intended as a substitute for professional advice or guidance. Readers are encouraged to seek support from qualified professionals as needed.

Chapter 1: Introduction

Navigating Male-Dominated Industries

Navigating male-dominated industries requires a blend of resilience, strategy, and confidence. In these professional landscapes, women often encounter unique challenges, from subtle biases to overt discrimination. However, with the right approach, individuals can not only succeed but also drive positive change within these environments. This introduction sets the stage for exploring the strategies and tactics essential for thriving in male-dominated industries, empowering individuals to navigate these complex landscapes with grace and determination.

Embracing Your Role as a Girl-Boss

Embracing your role as a "Girl-Boss" encapsulates a powerful ethos of leadership, ambition, and self-empowerment. In a world where gender norms and expectations often shape professional narratives, the concept of being a Girl-Boss redefines success on one's own terms. It's about owning your strengths, amplifying your voice, and forging paths that inspire others to do the same. By embracing this identity, individuals cultivate a mindset of resilience, innovation, and unwavering determination, fostering a community of trailblazers who challenge conventional wisdom and pave the way for a more inclusive and equitable future.

Chapter 2: Challenging Gender Stereotypes

Challenging gender stereotypes is not just about breaking moulds; it's about reshaping perceptions and fostering inclusivity in every aspect of life. These stereotypes often confine individuals to predefined roles based on their gender, limiting opportunities and perpetuating inequality. By challenging these norms, we dismantle barriers and create space for everyone to thrive based on their abilities, passions, and aspirations rather than their gender. It's a journey that requires courage, empathy, and solidarity— a commitment to questioning assumptions, advocating for change, and celebrating diversity in all its forms. Through collective action and unwavering determination, we can create a world where gender stereotypes are relics of the past, and every individual is free to define their own path without limitations.

Recognizing and Overcoming Bias and Discrimination

Challenging gender stereotypes is a multifaceted endeavour that involves recognizing, addressing, and overcoming biases and discrimination deeply ingrained in society. Here's an in-depth exploration:

Understanding Gender Stereotypes: Gender stereotypes are deeply rooted societal beliefs about the roles, behaviours, and attributes deemed appropriate for individuals based on their gender. These stereotypes often perpetuate harmful ideas, such as associating women with nurturing roles and men with leadership or dominance.

Recognizing Bias and Discrimination: Bias and discrimination based on gender can manifest in various forms, including unequal opportunities in education and employment, wage disparities, limited representation in leadership positions, and gender-based violence. It's crucial to recognize these biases and their impacts on individuals and society as a whole.

Promoting Awareness and Education: Education is a powerful tool for challenging gender stereotypes. By promoting awareness of these issues through workshops, discussions, and educational programs, individuals can better understand the complexity of gender dynamics and their effects on people's lives.

Advocating for Gender Equality: Advocacy efforts play a pivotal role in challenging gender stereotypes and promoting gender equality. This includes advocating for policy changes that address gender-based discrimination, supporting initiatives that promote women's leadership and empowerment, and challenging gender norms in media and advertising.

Creating Inclusive Environments: Creating inclusive environments where all individuals feel valued and respected regardless of their gender is essential for challenging stereotypes. This involves fostering diverse and inclusive workplaces, schools, and communities where everyone has equal opportunities to thrive.

Encouraging Critical Thinking: Encouraging critical thinking about gender roles and stereotypes is crucial for challenging ingrained beliefs. By questioning societal norms and expectations, individuals can develop a more nuanced understanding of gender and its intersections with other aspects of identity.

Supporting Intersectional Approaches: Gender stereotypes intersect with other forms of discrimination, such as race, ethnicity, sexuality, and disability. It's essential to adopt intersectional approaches that recognize and address the complex ways in which different forms of oppression intersect and compound.

Being an Ally: Allies play a vital role in challenging gender stereotypes and promoting equality. By actively supporting and advocating for marginalized genders, allies can help create a more inclusive and equitable society.

Challenging gender stereotypes requires a collective effort and ongoing commitment to dismantling entrenched biases and creating a world where all individuals are free to express themselves authentically and pursue their aspirations without limitations.

Reframing Perceptions of Women in Leadership

Reframing perceptions of women in leadership involves challenging traditional notions of leadership and advocating for a more inclusive and equitable representation of women in positions of power. Here's how this can be achieved:

Highlighting Diverse Leadership Styles: Women often bring unique leadership styles to the table, characterized by qualities such as empathy, collaboration, and inclusivity. By highlighting the effectiveness of these diverse leadership approaches, we can challenge the stereotype that leadership is inherently masculine and expand the definition of what it means to be a successful leader.

Celebrating Women's Achievements: Recognizing and celebrating the achievements of women leaders across various fields helps to counteract stereotypes and demonstrate the value they bring to their organizations and communities. This can be done through awards, public recognition, and media representation that showcase women's leadership accomplishments.

Providing Mentorship and Support: Mentorship and support programs can help women develop the skills, confidence, and networks needed to advance into leadership positions. By pairing aspiring female leaders with experienced mentors and providing resources and guidance, organizations can help break down barriers to entry and promote gender diversity in leadership.

Addressing Bias and Stereotypes: Bias and stereotypes about women's leadership capabilities persist in many workplaces and industries. It's essential to address these biases head-on through education, training, and policies that promote fairness and equality. By raising awareness of unconscious bias and providing tools to mitigate its impact, organizations can create a more inclusive environment for women leaders to thrive.

Advocating for Structural Changes: Structural barriers, such as lack of access to opportunities, unequal pay, and limited representation in decision-making bodies, hinder women's progress in leadership roles. Advocating for policy changes and organizational reforms that promote gender equity and level the playing field can help remove these obstacles and create pathways for women to ascend to leadership positions.

Building a Supportive Culture: Cultivating a workplace culture that values diversity, equity, and inclusion is essential for supporting women in leadership roles. This involves fostering an environment where all employees feel respected, heard, and valued, regardless of their gender. By promoting a culture of support and collaboration, organizations can empower women to excel as leaders.

Encouraging Female Leadership Development: Investing in female leadership development programs and initiatives helps to nurture the next generation of women leaders. By providing opportunities for skill-building, networking, and professional growth, organizations can empower women to overcome barriers and advance in their careers.

Reframing perceptions of women in leadership requires a concerted effort from individuals, organizations, and society as a whole. By challenging stereotypes, providing support and opportunities, and advocating for gender equity, we can create a more inclusive and diverse leadership landscape where women can thrive.

Chapter 3: Cultivating Confidence and Assertiveness

Cultivating confidence and assertiveness as a Girl-Boss is not just about leadership; it's a transformative mindset that empowers women to embrace their strengths, voice their ideas, and navigate the professional world with resilience and self-assurance. In a landscape where gender biases persist, cultivating these qualities becomes essential for women to assert their presence, break through barriers, and lead with authenticity. This introduction sets the stage for exploring how embracing confidence and assertiveness can not only propel individual success but also inspire a new generation of female leaders to challenge norms, shatter glass ceilings, and redefine the landscape of leadership on their terms.

Owning Your Voice and Value

Cultivating confidence and assertiveness as a Girl-Boss involves several key components, each contributing to the development of a strong, empowered leader. Breaking down this process into distinct sections facilitates a deeper understanding of the strategies and practices involved.

Recognizing Your Worth: The foundation of cultivating confidence and assertiveness lies in recognizing your inherent value. This involves acknowledging your skills, expertise, and unique perspective. Take stock of your achievements and strengths, understanding that they contribute to your worth as a leader. Reflect on past successes and challenges, recognizing the resilience and determination that have brought you to where you are today.

Embracing Your Voice: Owning your voice is about embracing your unique perspective and speaking up with confidence. Cultivate self-awareness to understand your values, passions, and goals, allowing you to articulate your ideas with clarity and conviction. Practice assertive communication techniques, such as using clear language, maintaining eye contact, and speaking with authority. Embrace opportunities to share your insights and opinions, whether in meetings, presentations, or networking events, demonstrating your confidence in your abilities.

Setting Boundaries: Assertiveness involves setting and maintaining boundaries to protect your time, energy, and well-being. Clearly communicate your expectations and limits to others, advocating for yourself and your needs. Learn to say no assertively, without guilt or apology, when requests or demands exceed your capacity or priorities. Prioritize self-care and balance, recognizing that maintaining boundaries is essential for long-term success and fulfilment as a leader.

Overcoming Self-Doubt: Confidence-building is often hindered by self-doubt and imposter syndrome. Challenge negative self-talk and limiting beliefs, replacing them with affirmations and positive self-statements. Seek support from mentors, peers, or professional development resources to gain perspective and build resilience. Celebrate your achievements and progress, recognizing that growth often comes from stepping outside your comfort zone and embracing new challenges.

Continuous Growth and Learning: Cultivating confidence and assertiveness is an ongoing process that requires commitment to personal and professional growth. Seek out opportunities for learning and development, whether through formal education, training programs, or hands-on experience. Embrace feedback as a tool for improvement, using it to refine your skills and enhance your leadership effectiveness. Stay open to new ideas and perspectives, recognizing that continuous learning is essential for adapting to evolving challenges and opportunities.

By breaking down the process of cultivating confidence and assertiveness into these distinct sections, women can develop the skills, mindset, and resilience needed to thrive as Girl-Bosses in any professional setting. Through self-awareness, assertive communication, boundary-setting, overcoming self-doubt, and continuous growth, women can confidently own their voice and value as leaders, driving positive change and inspiring others to do the same.

Assertive Communication Strategies for Success

Assertive communication is a cornerstone of success in any professional setting, enabling individuals to express their thoughts, needs, and boundaries effectively while maintaining respect for others. Here are key strategies for mastering assertive communication:

Clear and Direct Expression: Articulate your thoughts and feelings in a clear, direct manner, avoiding ambiguity or passive language. Use "I" statements to express your perspective without attributing blame or judgment to others. For example, instead of saying, "You never listen to my ideas," say, "I feel frustrated when I don't feel heard during our discussions."

Active Listening: Actively listen to others' perspectives without interrupting or formulating a response prematurely. Demonstrate empathy and understanding by paraphrasing their points and validating their feelings. This fosters a collaborative atmosphere where all parties feel heard and valued.

Setting Boundaries: Clearly communicate your boundaries and limits to others, asserting your needs and priorities. Use assertive language to express your boundaries without apologizing or justifying your decisions. For example, say, "I'm unable to take on additional projects at this time," rather than making excuses or feeling guilty for declining.

Respectful Assertiveness: Assert your opinions and preferences while respecting the rights and perspectives of others. Avoid aggressive or passive-aggressive communication styles, which can undermine relationships and create conflict. Maintain a calm and composed demeanour, even in challenging situations, to foster constructive dialogue and problem-solving.

Confidence and Self-Assurance: Project confidence and self-assurance through your body language, tone of voice, and demeanour. Stand tall, make eye contact, and speak with conviction to convey your message effectively. Trust in your abilities and value as a contributor, which will resonate with others and enhance your credibility.

Conflict Resolution Skills: Develop effective conflict resolution skills to address disagreements or misunderstandings assertively and constructively. Focus on finding mutually beneficial solutions rather than assigning blame or escalating tensions. Practice active listening, empathy, and compromise to navigate conflicts with professionalism and respect.

Practice and Feedback: Continuously refine your assertive communication skills through practice and feedback. Seek opportunities to assert yourself in various professional contexts, such as meetings, negotiations, or presentations. Reflect on your experiences and solicit feedback from trusted colleagues or mentors to identify areas for improvement and growth.

By mastering these assertive communication strategies, individuals can enhance their effectiveness, build stronger relationships, and navigate professional challenges with confidence and success. Assertive communication fosters a culture of mutual respect, collaboration, and accountability, empowering individuals to achieve their goals and contribute positively to their organizations.

Chapter 4: Building a Supportive Network

Building a supportive network is essential for personal and professional growth, providing opportunities for collaboration, mentorship, and mutual encouragement. In today's interconnected world, having a strong network of colleagues, mentors, and peers can offer invaluable support, guidance, and resources to navigate challenges, seize opportunities, and achieve goals. By cultivating meaningful relationships and fostering a community of support, individuals can access diverse perspectives, share knowledge and experiences, and build confidence and resilience in their pursuits. Whether in the workplace, industry associations, or online communities, building a supportive network is key to fostering success, fulfilment, and a sense of belonging in both personal and professional endeavours.

Finding Mentorship and Sponsorship Opportunities

Finding mentorship and sponsorship opportunities is crucial for personal and professional growth as a Girl-Boss. Here's a breakdown of strategies to seek and cultivate these relationships:

Clarify Your Goals: Before seeking mentors or sponsors, clarify your goals and what you hope to gain from the relationship. Whether it's career advancement, skill development, or guidance on work-life balance, having clear objectives will help you identify the right mentors and sponsors who can support your aspirations.

Seek Diverse Perspectives: Look for mentors and sponsors who offer diverse perspectives and experiences that align with your goals and values. Consider individuals from different industries, backgrounds, and levels of seniority who can provide valuable insights and broaden your horizons.

Utilize Professional Networks: Leverage your professional networks, both online and offline, to identify potential mentors and sponsors. Attend industry events, conferences, and networking mixers to connect with seasoned professionals who can offer guidance and support. Join professional organizations or online communities focused on women's leadership and entrepreneurship to expand your network further.

Formal Mentorship Programs: Many organizations offer formal mentorship programs designed to pair junior employees with more experienced mentors. Explore internal mentorship programs within your company or industry associations that facilitate mentorship connections. These programs often provide structured guidance and resources to support your professional development.

Initiate Relationships: Don't be afraid to initiate relationships with potential mentors and sponsors. Reach out via email or LinkedIn to express your admiration for their work and request an informational interview or coffee meeting. Come prepared with specific questions and topics to discuss, demonstrating your enthusiasm and commitment to learning from their expertise.

Build Trust and Rapport: Cultivate trust and rapport with your mentors and sponsors by being authentic, respectful, and receptive to feedback. Share your goals, challenges, and successes openly, allowing them to provide personalized guidance and support. Show appreciation for their time and insights, and be proactive in following up on their advice and recommendations.

Pay It Forward: As you progress in your career, consider paying it forward by serving as a mentor or sponsor to others. Sharing your knowledge and experiences not only benefits mentees but also strengthens your own leadership skills and networks. Actively seek out opportunities to support and empower aspiring Girl-Bosses, creating a culture of mentorship and mutual growth.

By actively seeking out mentorship and sponsorship opportunities, Girl-Bosses can access valuable guidance, support, and resources to advance their careers and achieve their goals. These relationships provide invaluable insights, encouragement, and networking opportunities that can propel women to new heights of success and leadership.

Creating a Community of Empowered Women

Creating a community of empowered women as a Girl-Boss is a powerful way to foster collaboration, support, and collective growth. Here's a breakdown of strategies to cultivate such a community:

Define Your Mission and Values: Clearly define the mission and values of your community, articulating its purpose and goals. Whether it's advancing women's leadership, promoting gender equality, or providing support for female entrepreneurs, establishing a shared vision will attract like-minded individuals who resonate with your cause.

Provide Resources and Support: Offer resources, tools, and support networks to empower women in their personal and professional endeavours. This could include mentorship programs, skills workshops, networking events, and online forums where members can connect, learn, and collaborate. Create a platform for sharing knowledge, experiences, and opportunities, facilitating mutual support and growth.

Foster Inclusivity and Diversity: Cultivate an inclusive and diverse community that welcomes women from all backgrounds, experiences, and perspectives. Ensure that everyone feels valued, respected, and represented, regardless of factors such as race, ethnicity, sexuality, or socioeconomic status. Embrace intersectionality and celebrate the unique contributions and identities of each member.

Encourage Collaboration and Networking: Create opportunities for collaboration and networking among community members, facilitating connections and partnerships that drive collective impact. Organize events, mastermind groups, and peer-to-peer support circles where women can share ideas, seek advice, and collaborate on projects or initiatives.

Encourage members to leverage each other's strengths and expertise, fostering a culture of reciprocity and mutual empowerment.

Celebrate Achievements and Milestones: Recognize and celebrate the achievements and milestones of community members, highlighting their successes and contributions. Showcase their stories and accomplishments through social media, newsletters, or events, inspiring others and reinforcing a culture of support and encouragement. Create space for women to share their successes, challenges, and lessons learned, fostering a sense of camaraderie and solidarity.

Promote Leadership and Mentorship: Encourage leadership development and mentorship within the community, empowering women to step into leadership roles and support each other's growth and development. Provide opportunities for members to mentor and be mentored, fostering a culture of knowledge-sharing, guidance, and mentorship. Invest in leadership training, coaching, and skill-building programs to equip women with the tools and confidence they need to lead effectively.

Amplify Voices and Advocacy: Amplify the voices of community members and advocate for their needs and interests in broader conversations and spaces. Provide platforms for women to share their perspectives, ideas, and experiences, amplifying their voices and advocating for change. Engage in advocacy efforts and initiatives that address systemic barriers and inequalities, leveraging the collective power of the community to drive positive social change.

By creating a community of empowered women, Girl-Bosses can harness the collective strength, wisdom, and support of like-minded individuals to effect meaningful change and advance their shared goals. Together, they can inspire, uplift, and empower each other to thrive personally and professionally, forging a brighter and more equitable future for women everywhere.

Chapter 5: Embracing Your Unique Strengths

Embracing your unique strengths as a Girl-Boss is a transformative journey of self-discovery and empowerment, where authenticity becomes your greatest asset. In a world that often emphasizes conformity, recognizing and celebrating your individual strengths, talents, and perspectives is a powerful act of self-affirmation. As a Girl-Boss, embracing your uniqueness allows you to harness your distinct voice, vision, and experiences to drive innovation, inspire others, and create meaningful impact. By embracing your authentic self and leveraging your strengths, you not only unlock your full potential as a leader but also pave the way for greater diversity, inclusion, and authenticity in leadership.

Leveraging Female Leadership Traits

Embracing your unique strengths and leveraging female leadership traits as a Girl-Boss is a powerful strategy for success in today's dynamic professional landscape. Here's how to harness these qualities effectively:

Emotional Intelligence: Women often excel in emotional intelligence, which involves understanding and managing emotions, both your own and others'. Use your empathy and intuition to build strong relationships, foster collaboration, and navigate complex interpersonal dynamics. Recognize the value of emotional intelligence in leadership, as it enables you to connect with and inspire your team on a deeper level.

Communication Skills: Women are often adept communicators, skilled at articulating ideas, active listening, and fostering open dialogue. Leverage these communication skills to convey your vision, motivate your team, and build a positive organizational culture. Foster a supportive environment where everyone feels heard, valued, and empowered to contribute their ideas and perspectives.

Collaborative Leadership Style: Embrace a collaborative leadership style that values teamwork, consensus-building, and inclusivity. Recognize the strengths and expertise of your team members, and empower them to take ownership of projects and initiatives. Cultivate a culture of trust, respect, and mutual support, where everyone feels encouraged to share their ideas and work together towards common goals.

Resilience and Adaptability: Women often demonstrate resilience and adaptability in the face of challenges and setbacks. Draw upon your resilience to navigate uncertainty, overcome obstacles, and lead your team through times of change and adversity. Embrace a growth mindset that views challenges as opportunities for learning and growth, and inspire others to do the same.

Empowerment and Mentorship: As a female leader, prioritize empowerment and mentorship, both for yourself and others. Advocate for the advancement of women in your organization and industry, and actively mentor and sponsor emerging leaders. Create opportunities for women to develop their skills, build confidence, and advance their careers, fostering a pipeline of future leaders who will continue to drive positive change.

Authenticity and Integrity: Lead with authenticity and integrity, staying true to your values, principles, and convictions. Be transparent and honest in your interactions, and lead by example through your actions and decisions. Cultivate a culture of trust and accountability, where ethical conduct and integrity are non-negotiables.

Continuous Learning and Growth: Embrace a mindset of continuous learning and growth, recognizing that leadership is a journey of discovery and development. Invest in your own professional development through training, coaching, and networking opportunities. Stay curious, open-minded, and adaptable, and seek out feedback and mentorship to support your ongoing growth as a leader.

By embracing your unique strengths and leveraging female leadership traits, you can inspire others, drive positive change, and make a lasting impact as a Girl-Boss. Lead with empathy, authenticity, and resilience, and empower others to do the same, creating a more inclusive, equitable, and empowering workplace for all.

Finding Your Leadership Style and Voice

Finding your leadership style and voice as a Girl-Boss is an empowering journey of self-discovery and authenticity. Here's how to navigate this process effectively:

Reflect on Your Values and Goals: Take time to reflect on your values, passions, and long-term goals. What matters most to you? What kind of leader do you aspire to be? Clarifying your values and goals will provide a foundation for developing your leadership style and voice aligned with your authentic self.

Identify Your Strengths and Weaknesses: Conduct a self-assessment to identify your strengths, weaknesses, and areas for growth. What are you naturally good at? Where do you struggle? Understanding your strengths will allow you to leverage them effectively in your leadership style, while acknowledging your weaknesses will help you identify opportunities for development.

Explore Different Leadership Styles: Familiarize yourself with various leadership styles, from visionary and transformational to servant and democratic. Consider the strengths and weaknesses of each style and how they align with your values, personality, and goals. Experiment with different approaches to leadership to determine what feels most authentic and effective for you.

Embrace Your Authenticity: Authenticity is key to finding your leadership voice. Embrace your unique personality, experiences, and perspective, and allow them to shine through in your leadership style. Be genuine, transparent, and true to yourself in your interactions with others, inspiring trust, respect, and loyalty.

Develop Your Communication Skills: Effective communication is essential for expressing your leadership voice and inspiring others. Hone your communication skills, both verbal and nonverbal, to convey your ideas, vision, and expectations clearly and persuasively. Practice active listening, empathy, and clarity in your communication to foster understanding and connection with your team.

Lead by Example: Lead by example by demonstrating the values and behaviours you wish to see in others. Model integrity, accountability, and resilience in your actions and decisions, inspiring others to follow suit. Be consistent in your words and actions, earning the trust and respect of your team through your leadership.

Seek Feedback and Growth: Continuously seek feedback from others on your leadership style and voice, and be open to constructive criticism and opportunities for growth. Actively solicit input from your team members, mentors, and peers, and use their insights to refine and improve your leadership approach over time.

Empower Others: Empower others to find their own leadership style and voice by creating a supportive and inclusive environment where everyone feels valued and empowered to contribute. Encourage diversity of thought, foster collaboration and innovation, and celebrate the unique strengths and talents of each team member.

By intentionally exploring your values, strengths, and goals, embracing authenticity, developing your communication skills, leading by example, seeking feedback and growth, and empowering others, you can find your leadership style and voice as a Girl-Boss that resonates with who you are and inspires others to greatness.

Chapter 6: Overcoming Imposter Syndrome

Overcoming imposter syndrome as a Girl-Boss is a liberating journey of self-acceptance and empowerment, where you challenge the internalized doubt and fear that undermine your confidence and accomplishments. Despite your achievements and capabilities, imposter syndrome can make you feel like a fraud, questioning your worthiness and abilities in your leadership role. Recognizing and addressing these feelings is essential for unleashing your full potential and embracing your unique contributions as a leader. By cultivating self-awareness, reframing negative thoughts, and seeking support from mentors and peers, you can overcome imposter syndrome and step into your power with authenticity, resilience, and self-assurance, ultimately thriving in your leadership journey.

Recognizing and Overcoming Self-Doubt

Recognizing and overcoming self-doubt is a critical aspect of personal and professional growth for Girl-Bosses. Here's how to address this challenge effectively:

Acknowledge Your Feelings: The first step in overcoming self-doubt is to acknowledge and accept your feelings without judgment. Recognize that it's normal to experience self-doubt from time to time, especially when facing new challenges or stepping outside your comfort zone.

Challenge Negative Self-Talk: Pay attention to your inner dialogue and challenge negative self-talk that undermines your confidence and self-belief. Replace self-critical thoughts with positive affirmations and reminders of your strengths, accomplishments, and past successes.

Set Realistic Expectations: Set realistic expectations for yourself and recognize that perfection is unattainable. Embrace the concept of "progress, not perfection," and celebrate your achievements and progress, no matter how small.

Focus on Your Strengths: Shift your focus from your weaknesses and limitations to your strengths and abilities. Identify your unique talents, skills, and qualities that contribute to your success as a leader, and leverage them to overcome challenges and achieve your goals.

Seek Support and Validation: Surround yourself with supportive friends, family members, mentors, and peers who believe in you and your potential. Seek validation and encouragement from trusted individuals who can offer perspective and support during times of doubt.

Take Action Despite Fear: Take action despite your fears and insecurities, and embrace the discomfort that comes with growth and change. Recognize that courage is not the absence of fear but the willingness to act in spite of it.

Practice Self-Compassion: Practice self-compassion and kindness towards yourself, especially during moments of self-doubt and vulnerability. Treat yourself with the same kindness and understanding that you would offer to a friend facing similar challenges.

Focus on Learning and Growth: Embrace a growth mindset that views challenges and setbacks as opportunities for learning and growth. Approach each obstacle as a chance to develop new skills, gain valuable experience, and become a stronger, more resilient leader.

Celebrate Your Achievements: Celebrate your achievements, no matter how small, and acknowledge your progress along the way. Keep a journal or gratitude list to reflect on your accomplishments and remind yourself of your capabilities.

Seek Professional Help if Needed: If self-doubt significantly impacts your well-being or ability to function, consider seeking support from a therapist, coach, or counsellor who can provide guidance and tools to overcome self-doubt and build self-confidence.

By recognizing and addressing self-doubt with compassion, courage, and resilience, Girl-Bosses can unlock their full potential and confidently pursue their dreams and aspirations. Remember that self-doubt is a natural part of the journey to success, and with the right mindset and support, it can be overcome.

Celebrating Your Achievements and Abilities

Celebrating your achievements and abilities as a Girl-Boss is not just about recognizing your accomplishments; it's about embracing your journey, honouring your growth, and inspiring others along the way. Here's how to celebrate your success authentically:

Acknowledge Your Accomplishments: Take the time to acknowledge and appreciate your achievements, no matter how big or small. Celebrate the milestones you've reached and the goals you've accomplished, recognizing the hard work, dedication, and resilience it took to get there.

Share Your Successes: Don't be afraid to share your successes with others. Share your accomplishments on social media, in team meetings, or with friends and family. By sharing your journey, you not only inspire others but also reaffirm your own achievements and abilities.

Reflect on Your Growth: Take time to reflect on your growth and development as a leader. Look back on where you started and how far you've come, acknowledging the lessons learned and challenges overcome along the way. Celebrate the personal and professional growth you've experienced, recognizing that each experience has shaped you into the leader you are today.

Celebrate Others' Successes: Celebrate the successes of those around you, whether it's your team members, colleagues, or peers. Recognize their accomplishments and contributions, and celebrate their victories as if they were your own. By fostering a culture of celebration and support, you create a positive and uplifting environment where everyone feels valued and appreciated.

Treat Yourself: Treat yourself to something special as a reward for your hard work and dedication. Whether it's a spa day, a fancy dinner, or a weekend getaway, take the time to indulge and pamper yourself for all that you've achieved. Celebrate your success and honor yourself for your accomplishments.

Express Gratitude: Express gratitude for the support and encouragement you've received along the way. Thank your mentors, supporters, and team members for their guidance, mentorship, and belief in you. Let them know how much their support has meant to you and how it has contributed to your success.

Set New Goals: After celebrating your achievements, set new goals and aspirations to continue challenging yourself and growing as a leader. Embrace new opportunities and challenges with enthusiasm and determination, knowing that you have the skills, abilities, and resilience to succeed.

Inspire Others: Use your success as a platform to inspire and empower others. Share your story, insights, and lessons learned to encourage others to pursue their dreams and goals. Be a role model for aspiring Girl-Bosses, showing them what's possible when you believe in yourself and work hard to achieve your dreams.

By celebrating your achievements and abilities as a Girl-Boss, you not only honour your own journey but also inspire others to believe in themselves and pursue their own paths to success. Remember to celebrate the moments of triumph, big and small, and never underestimate the power of your own accomplishments to inspire and uplift those around you.

Chapter 7: Negotiating Like a Pro

Negotiating like a pro is a strategic art form that involves mastering the skills of communication, persuasion, and compromise to achieve favourable outcomes in various situations. Whether it's negotiating a salary, contract terms, or business deals, honing your negotiation skills is essential for asserting your value and advocating for your interests effectively. By understanding your goals, preparing thoroughly, and adopting a collaborative yet assertive approach, you can navigate negotiations with confidence and professionalism, ultimately securing mutually beneficial agreements and advancing your personal and professional objectives. Whether you're a seasoned negotiator or just starting out, embracing negotiation as a skill to be developed and refined can empower you to thrive in diverse contexts and seize opportunities for success.

Strategies for Successful Salary Negotiations

Negotiating salary with your team can be a delicate process, but with the right strategies, it can lead to a fair and mutually beneficial outcome. Here are some steps to navigate successful salary negotiations:

Research Market Rates: Before entering negotiations, research industry standards and market rates for similar roles in your region. Websites like Glassdoor, PayScale, and LinkedIn Salary can provide valuable insights into salary ranges for comparable positions. Having this data at hand will strengthen your negotiation position and provide evidence to support your requests.

Know Your Value: Understand your worth within the organization based on your skills, experience, and contributions. Reflect on your accomplishments, performance reviews, and any additional responsibilities you've taken on since your last salary review. Be prepared to articulate your value to the team and how your contributions justify your desired salary increase.

Identify Your Priorities: Clarify your financial priorities and desired compensation package beyond just salary, such as bonuses, benefits, equity, or professional development opportunities. Consider what is most important to you and be prepared to negotiate on multiple fronts to achieve a satisfactory outcome.

Prepare Your Pitch: Develop a compelling pitch that outlines your accomplishments, skills, and the value you bring to the team. Practice articulating your points confidently and concisely, emphasizing the benefits to the organization of meeting your salary expectations. Anticipate potential objections or counterarguments and prepare responses in advance.

Timing is Key: Choose the right timing for initiating salary negotiations. Ideally, schedule a meeting with your manager when you have recently achieved significant accomplishments or completed a successful project. Avoid waiting until your annual performance review, as salary decisions may already be predetermined at that point.

Frame the Conversation Positively: Approach the negotiation as a collaborative discussion aimed at finding a mutually beneficial solution. Express gratitude for the opportunity to contribute to the team and highlight your enthusiasm for continuing to grow and excel in your role. Emphasize your commitment to the organization's success and your desire to be fairly compensated for your contributions.

Be Flexible and Open-Minded: Be open to compromise and flexible in your negotiations. Consider alternative forms of compensation or perks if your salary request cannot be fully met. Keep an open mind and focus on achieving a solution that satisfies both parties and maintains a positive working relationship.

Follow-Up in Writing: After reaching an agreement, summarize the key points of the negotiation in writing, including the agreed-upon salary, benefits, and any other terms discussed. This helps prevent misunderstandings and ensures clarity moving forward.

Continue to Advocate for Yourself: Salary negotiations are not a one-time event. Continue to monitor your performance, market trends, and opportunities for advancement within the organization. Advocate for yourself regularly and be proactive in seeking opportunities for salary increases or promotions as your contributions and responsibilities evolve.

By employing these strategies, you can navigate successful salary negotiations with your team, ensuring that you are fairly compensated for your skills, experience, and contributions while maintaining positive working relationships with your colleagues and supervisors.

Assertive Negotiation Techniques for Career Advancement

Assertive negotiation techniques are essential for career advancement, enabling individuals to advocate for themselves effectively and secure opportunities for growth and advancement. Here are some assertive negotiation techniques to employ:

Know Your Value: Before entering negotiations, thoroughly research your market value and understand the worth of your skills, experience, and contributions to the organization. Use data and evidence to support your assertions, demonstrating why you deserve the compensation or opportunities you are seeking.

Set Clear Goals: Define your objectives and priorities for the negotiation, whether it's a salary increase, promotion, additional responsibilities, or professional development opportunities. Establish clear and specific goals that align with your long-term career aspirations and desired outcomes.

Prepare Thoroughly: Prepare for negotiations by anticipating potential objections, concerns, or questions that may arise. Develop persuasive arguments and evidence to address these points and support your position effectively. Practice articulating your points confidently and succinctly to enhance your negotiation skills.

Focus on Win-Win Solutions: Approach negotiations with a collaborative mindset, seeking mutually beneficial outcomes that address the needs and interests of both parties. Emphasize the value you bring to the organization and how meeting your requests will contribute to its success and growth. Look for creative solutions and compromises that satisfy both sides.

Communicate Assertively: Assertive communication is key to successful negotiations. Clearly and confidently articulate your needs, preferences, and boundaries, using assertive language and body language to convey your message effectively. Maintain eye contact, speak clearly and directly, and avoid apologizing or hedging your statements.

Listen Actively: Actively listen to the other party's perspective and concerns, demonstrating empathy and understanding. Ask clarifying questions and paraphrase their points to ensure mutual understanding. By listening attentively, you can identify common ground, areas for compromise, and opportunities for collaboration.

Stay Calm and Composed: Maintain a calm and composed demeanour throughout the negotiation, even in the face of challenges or disagreements. Avoid becoming defensive or emotional, and focus on maintaining a professional and respectful tone. Keep your emotions in check and stay focused on the objectives of the negotiation.

Be Prepared to Walk Away: Know your limits and be prepared to walk away from the negotiation if the terms are not favourable or if your needs are not being met. Having a clear alternative or "Plan B" can give you leverage in negotiations and prevent you from accepting terms that are not in your best interest.

Follow Up in Writing: After reaching an agreement, summarize the key points of the negotiation in writing and confirm any commitments made by both parties. This helps prevent misunderstandings and ensures clarity moving forward.

By employing assertive negotiation techniques, individuals can advocate for themselves effectively, secure opportunities for career advancement, and achieve their professional goals with confidence and success.

Chapter 8: Balancing Ambition with Self-Care

Balancing ambition with self-care is a delicate yet vital endeavour that requires prioritizing both professional goals and personal well-being to foster long-term success and fulfilment. While ambition propels us to strive for excellence and pursue our aspirations, neglecting self-care can lead to burnout, stress, and diminished productivity. By cultivating self-awareness, setting boundaries, and integrating self-care practices into our daily lives, we can sustain our ambition while nurturing our physical, mental, and emotional health. Recognizing that self-care is not a luxury but a necessity for sustainable success, finding harmony between ambition and self-care allows us to achieve our goals with greater resilience, clarity, and balance, ultimately leading to a more fulfilling and meaningful life journey.

Prioritizing Work-Life Balance

Prioritizing work-life balance is essential for maintaining overall well-being, reducing stress, and achieving long-term success and fulfilment in both personal and professional spheres. Here are some strategies to help prioritize work-life balance:

Set Boundaries: Establish clear boundaries between work and personal life by defining specific times for work and leisure activities. Communicate these boundaries to your colleagues, managers, and clients to manage expectations and prevent work from encroaching on personal time.

Manage Time Effectively: Prioritize tasks and allocate time efficiently to accomplish your work responsibilities while leaving room for leisure, relaxation, and self-care. Use time-management techniques such as prioritization, delegation, and scheduling to maximize productivity and minimize stress.

Practice Self-Care: Make self-care a priority by engaging in activities that nourish your mind, body, and spirit. This may include exercise, meditation, hobbies, spending time with loved ones, or pursuing creative interests. Prioritize activities that rejuvenate and energize you, helping you to recharge and maintain resilience in the face of work-related challenges.

Set Realistic Expectations: Be realistic about what you can accomplish within a given timeframe and avoid overcommitting yourself. Set achievable goals and deadlines, and be willing to renegotiate deadlines or delegate tasks when necessary to prevent burnout and maintain balance.

Communicate Openly: Communicate openly with your colleagues, managers, and clients about your work-life balance needs and priorities. Be transparent about your availability, boundaries, and limitations, and advocate for support and flexibility when needed. Cultivate a culture of mutual respect and understanding within your workplace that values work-life balance as essential for employee well-being and productivity.

Unplug and Disconnect: Take regular breaks from work and disconnect from technology to recharge and rejuvenate. Set aside designated times to unplug from email, phone calls, and work-related responsibilities, allowing yourself to fully disengage and focus on personal activities and relationships.

Delegate and Outsource: Delegate tasks and responsibilities to others whenever possible, both at work and at home. Identify tasks that can be outsourced or automated to free up time and mental energy for activities that are more meaningful or enjoyable.

Set Aside Time for Reflection: Schedule regular time for reflection and self-assessment to evaluate your work-life balance and make adjustments as needed. Consider what activities bring you joy and fulfilment, and identify areas where you may need to reallocate time or resources to achieve greater balance and satisfaction.

Seek Support: Reach out to friends, family members, colleagues, or professionals for support and guidance in prioritizing work-life balance. Share your challenges and experiences with others, and seek advice or encouragement from those who have successfully achieved balance in their own lives.

By implementing these strategies, individuals can prioritize work-life balance, reduce stress, and cultivate a more fulfilling and sustainable approach to both work and personal life. Remember that achieving work-life balance is an ongoing process that requires self-awareness, intentionality, and commitment to prioritizing what truly matters in life.

Setting Boundaries and Practicing Self-Compassion

Setting boundaries and practicing self-compassion are essential components of maintaining overall well-being and achieving a healthy work-life balance. Here's how to effectively set boundaries and cultivate self-compassion:

Identify Your Needs: Start by identifying your needs and priorities in both your personal and professional life. What activities or commitments are essential to your well-being? What are your non-negotiable boundaries in terms of time, energy, and resources? Understanding your needs will help you establish clear boundaries that support your overall health and happiness.

Communicate Your Boundaries: Clearly communicate your boundaries to others, including colleagues, managers, friends, and family members. Be assertive in expressing your needs and limits, and set realistic expectations for how you will allocate your time and energy. Use assertive communication techniques to convey your boundaries respectfully and effectively.

Practice Saying No: Learn to say no to requests or commitments that do not align with your priorities or values. It's okay to decline invitations, delegate tasks, or set limits on your availability when necessary to protect your time and well-being. Prioritize activities that bring you joy, fulfilment, and meaning, and be selective about where you invest your time and energy.

Create Physical and Emotional Space: Establish physical and emotional boundaries to create space for self-care, relaxation, and reflection. Designate specific times and places for work-related activities, and set aside uninterrupted time for leisure, hobbies, and personal interests. Create boundaries around technology use and screen time to prevent work from encroaching on personal time.

Practice Self-Compassion: Cultivate self-compassion by treating yourself with kindness, understanding, and acceptance, especially during times of stress or difficulty. Recognize that it's okay to make mistakes, experience setbacks, or fall short of your own expectations. Practice self-care activities that nourish your mind, body, and spirit, and prioritize your own well-being as you would for a friend or loved one.

Set Realistic Expectations: Manage your expectations and avoid placing undue pressure on yourself to achieve perfection or meet unrealistic standards. Set realistic goals and deadlines that allow for flexibility, creativity, and balance. Focus on progress rather than perfection, and celebrate your achievements, no matter how small.

Establish Work-Life Boundaries: Create clear boundaries between your work and personal life to prevent burnout and maintain balance. Set specific work hours and stick to them, avoiding the temptation to check email or respond to work-related requests outside of designated times. Create rituals or routines to transition between work and leisure activities, such as a daily walk or meditation practice.

Seek Support and Guidance: Reach out to friends, family members, mentors, or professionals for support and guidance in setting boundaries and practicing self-compassion. Surround yourself with people who respect your boundaries and encourage you to prioritize your well-being. Consider seeking therapy or coaching if you need additional support in managing stress, anxiety, or other challenges related to boundary-setting and self-care.

By setting boundaries and practicing self-compassion, you can protect your well-being, reduce stress, and cultivate a more balanced and fulfilling life. Remember that boundary-setting and self-compassion are ongoing practices that require patience, self-awareness, and commitment to prioritizing your own needs and values.

Chapter 9: Leading with Empathy and Compassion

Leading with empathy and compassion is a transformative approach to leadership that prioritizes understanding, connection, and care for others. In a fast-paced and often impersonal world, leaders who embody empathy and compassion cultivate trust, loyalty, and collaboration within their teams and organizations. By actively listening, acknowledging others' perspectives, and showing genuine concern for their well-being, empathetic leaders foster a sense of belonging and psychological safety, empowering individuals to thrive and contribute their best work. Through empathy and compassion, leaders can inspire positive change, build resilient teams, and create a culture of kindness and inclusivity that transcends boundaries and fosters collective growth and success.

Building Stronger Teams Through Emotional Intelligence

Building stronger teams through emotional intelligence involves fostering an environment where team members can understand, manage, and empathize with their own emotions and those of others. Here are key strategies to cultivate emotional intelligence within your team:

Lead by Example: As a leader, model emotional intelligence by demonstrating self-awareness, empathy, and effective communication in your interactions with team members. Show vulnerability when appropriate and acknowledge your own emotions and reactions, setting a positive example for others to follow.

Emphasize Self-Awareness: Encourage team members to develop self-awareness by reflecting on their emotions, strengths, weaknesses, and communication styles. Provide opportunities for self-assessment and reflection, such as personality assessments or 360-degree feedback, to help team members gain insights into their own behaviours and tendencies.

Promote Empathy and Perspective-Taking: Foster empathy and perspective-taking among team members by encouraging them to understand and appreciate the feelings, perspectives, and experiences of others. Create opportunities for team members to share their stories, perspectives, and challenges, fostering a sense of connection and understanding within the team.

Cultivate Effective Communication Skills: Develop effective communication skills within the team, emphasizing active listening, clear expression, and constructive feedback. Encourage open and honest communication, where team members feel comfortable expressing their thoughts, feelings, and concerns without fear of judgment or reprisal.

Manage Conflict Constructively: Teach team members how to manage conflict constructively by addressing differences and disagreements with empathy, respect, and collaboration. Provide conflict resolution training and tools to help team members navigate conflicts and disagreements in a productive and respectful manner.

Encourage Collaboration and Teamwork: Foster a culture of collaboration and teamwork where team members support and uplift each other, rather than competing or working in isolation. Emphasize the importance of collective goals and shared success, encouraging team members to collaborate, share ideas, and leverage each other's strengths.

Provide Emotional Support and Recognition: Offer emotional support and recognition to team members for their contributions, efforts, and achievements. Celebrate successes, milestones, and accomplishments as a team, acknowledging the hard work and dedication of individual members. Provide opportunities for team members to express gratitude and appreciation for each other's efforts.

Offer Training and Development: Invest in training and development programs that focus on emotional intelligence, interpersonal skills, and relationship-building within the team. Provide resources, workshops, and coaching to help team members develop their emotional intelligence competencies and enhance their effectiveness as collaborators and leaders.

By prioritizing emotional intelligence within your team, you can create a culture of trust, collaboration, and mutual respect that fosters stronger relationships, enhances communication, and drives collective success. Emotional intelligence is not only essential for individual well-being and growth but also for building high-performing teams that thrive in today's dynamic and complex work environments.

Creating Inclusive and Supportive Work Environments

Creating inclusive and supportive work environments is crucial for fostering diversity, equity, and belonging within organizations. Here are key strategies to promote inclusivity and supportiveness in the workplace:

Establish a Clear Vision and Values: Define and communicate a clear vision and set of values that prioritize diversity, equity, and inclusion (DEI) within the organization. Articulate a commitment to creating a workplace where all individuals feel valued, respected, and empowered to contribute their unique perspectives and talents.

Promote Diversity in Hiring and Promotion: Implement inclusive hiring and promotion practices that prioritize diversity and representation at all levels of the organization. Adopt strategies to attract, recruit, and retain diverse talent, such as removing bias from job descriptions, implementing blind resume screening, and establishing diverse interview panels.

Provide Diversity and Inclusion Training: Offer training and education programs to increase awareness and understanding of diversity, equity, and inclusion issues among employees. Provide resources and workshops on topics such as unconscious bias, cultural competence, and inclusive leadership to help employees develop the knowledge and skills needed to create inclusive work environments.

Create Policies and Procedures that Support Inclusion: Review and revise organizational policies and procedures to ensure they promote diversity, equity, and inclusion. Implement policies that address issues such as equal pay, harassment prevention, accommodations for disabilities, and flexible work arrangements to support employees from diverse backgrounds and experiences.

Foster Psychological Safety: Cultivate a culture of psychological safety where employees feel comfortable speaking up, sharing ideas, and expressing their concerns without fear of retaliation or judgment. Encourage open communication, active listening, and constructive feedback to create an environment where all voices are heard and valued.

Offer Employee Resource Groups (ERGs): Establish Employee Resource Groups (ERGs) or affinity groups to provide support, networking, and professional development opportunities for employees from underrepresented backgrounds. These groups can serve as valuable forums for sharing experiences, fostering mentorship, and advocating for diversity and inclusion within the organization.

Provide Mentorship and Sponsorship Programs: Implement mentorship and sponsorship programs to support the professional development and advancement of employees from underrepresented groups. Pair employees with mentors and sponsors who can provide guidance, support, and advocacy to help them navigate their careers and overcome barriers to success.

Lead by Example: Demonstrate inclusive leadership behaviours by actively championing diversity, equity, and inclusion initiatives within the organization. Lead by example by modelling inclusive behaviours, engaging in open dialogue about DEI issues, and holding yourself and others accountable for creating a culture of respect and belonging.

Measure Progress and Hold Yourself Accountable: Establish metrics and key performance indicators (KPIs) to track progress on diversity, equity, and inclusion goals and initiatives. Regularly assess and evaluate the impact of DEI efforts, solicit feedback from employees, and adjust strategies as needed to ensure ongoing improvement and accountability.

By implementing these strategies, organizations can create inclusive and supportive work environments where all employees feel valued, respected, and empowered to contribute their best work. Prioritizing diversity, equity, and inclusion not only benefits individual employees but also drives innovation, engagement, and organizational success in the long run.

Chapter 10: Thriving in Leadership Roles

Thriving in leadership roles as a Girl-Boss is an empowering journey of self-discovery, growth, and impact, where women embrace their unique strengths and perspectives to drive positive change and success. In a landscape often dominated by traditional norms and expectations, Girl-Bosses bring fresh insights, innovative solutions, and authentic leadership styles to the table, challenging the status quo and redefining what it means to lead with purpose and authenticity. By cultivating resilience, confidence, and a supportive network of allies and mentors, women leaders can navigate challenges, seize opportunities, and create thriving environments where everyone can thrive and succeed. Through their leadership, Girl-Bosses inspire others to embrace their potential, break barriers, and make a meaningful impact in their organizations, industries, and communities.

Overcoming Challenges as a Female Leader

Overcoming challenges as a female leader requires resilience, determination, and strategic navigation of gender biases and systemic barriers. Here are key strategies to address common challenges faced by female leaders:

Build Confidence and Assertiveness: Cultivate confidence and assertiveness in your leadership style by recognizing your strengths, expertise, and value as a leader. Practice assertive communication techniques, set clear boundaries, and advocate for yourself and your ideas with conviction.

Navigate Gender Bias: Be aware of gender biases and stereotypes that may impact perceptions of female leaders, such as the "double bind" of being seen as either too assertive or too passive. Address bias directly by challenging stereotypes, advocating for equitable treatment, and highlighting your accomplishments and qualifications.

Seek Mentorship and Support: Find mentors and sponsors who can provide guidance, support, and advocacy as you navigate your leadership journey. Look for role models who have successfully overcome similar challenges and can offer insights and advice based on their experiences.

Build a Supportive Network: Surround yourself with a supportive network of peers, colleagues, and allies who can offer encouragement, advice, and solidarity. Join professional organizations, networking groups, and affinity groups that prioritize diversity, equity, and inclusion to connect with like-minded individuals and share resources and experiences.

Develop Resilience: Cultivate resilience to overcome setbacks, challenges, and obstacles encountered along the way. Embrace failure as an opportunity for growth and learning, and develop coping strategies to manage stress, uncertainty, and adversity effectively.

Advocate for Change: Use your position of leadership to advocate for systemic change and organizational policies that promote gender equity and inclusion. Champion initiatives such as pay equity, parental leave, flexible work arrangements, and diversity recruitment and retention efforts to create a more supportive and equitable workplace for all employees.

Lead by Example: Lead by example by demonstrating inclusive leadership behaviours and fostering a culture of respect, fairness, and belonging within your team and organization. Be intentional about promoting diversity, equity, and inclusion in your decision-making processes, hiring practices, and talent development efforts.

Leverage Your Unique Strengths: Embrace your unique strengths and leadership qualities as a woman, such as empathy, collaboration, and resilience. Capitalize on these strengths to build strong relationships, foster teamwork, and drive positive change within your organization.

Stay Committed to Your Goals: Stay committed to your goals and aspirations as a leader, even in the face of adversity or opposition. Remain focused on your vision and purpose, and draw inspiration from your passion and determination to make a difference in your organization and beyond.

By employing these strategies, female leaders can overcome challenges, break through barriers, and thrive in their roles, paving the way for greater gender equity and representation in leadership positions. Remember that resilience, support, and advocacy are essential for driving meaningful change and creating more inclusive and equitable workplaces for future generations of leaders.

Harnessing Your Leadership Potential for Positive Impact

Harnessing your leadership potential for positive impact involves leveraging your skills, influence, and vision to drive meaningful change and inspire others to reach their full potential. Here are key strategies to maximize your leadership impact:

Clarify Your Vision and Values: Define your personal and professional vision and values, reflecting on what matters most to you and the impact you want to have as a leader. Align your actions and decisions with your vision and values, serving as a guiding compass for your leadership journey.

Lead with Purpose: Lead with purpose by articulating a compelling vision for your team or organization that inspires others to join you in pursuit of a common goal. Communicate your purpose authentically and passionately, rallying others around a shared mission and motivating them to contribute their best efforts.

Develop Your Leadership Skills: Continuously invest in developing your leadership skills and capabilities through education, training, and self-improvement initiatives. Enhance your communication, decision-making, problem-solving, and emotional intelligence skills to become a more effective and influential leader.

Empower Others: Empower others to reach their full potential by fostering a culture of trust, autonomy, and accountability within your team or organization. Delegate authority, provide opportunities for growth and development, and recognize and celebrate the contributions of team members.

Lead by Example: Lead by example by embodying the qualities and behaviours you wish to see in others. Demonstrate integrity, authenticity, and resilience in your actions and decisions, earning the trust and respect of your team members and stakeholders.

Inspire and Motivate: Inspire and motivate others through your words and actions, encouraging them to embrace new challenges, pursue excellence, and achieve their goals. Share your passion, enthusiasm, and optimism for the future, and provide encouragement and support to those facing obstacles or setbacks.

Foster Collaboration and Diversity: Foster collaboration and diversity within your team or organization, recognizing the value of different perspectives, backgrounds, and experiences. Create opportunities for collaboration, innovation, and creativity by bringing together diverse teams and stakeholders to solve complex problems and drive positive change.

Lead with Empathy and Compassion: Lead with empathy and compassion by understanding and valuing the needs, concerns, and experiences of others. Listen actively, show empathy, and provide support and encouragement to those facing challenges or difficulties.

Measure and Evaluate Impact: Measure and evaluate the impact of your leadership efforts by setting goals, tracking progress, and soliciting feedback from others. Reflect on your successes and failures, learn from your experiences, and adjust your approach as needed to maximize your leadership impact.

Be a Lifelong Learner: Commit to lifelong learning and growth as a leader, seeking out new opportunities for development and self-improvement. Stay curious, open-minded, and adaptable, embracing change as an opportunity for growth and innovation.

By harnessing your leadership potential for positive impact, you can inspire and empower others, drive meaningful change, and contribute to the greater good of your organization, community, and society as a whole. Remember that leadership is not just about achieving personal success but about making a difference in the lives of others and leaving a lasting legacy of positive change.

Chapter 11: Advocating for Gender Equality

Advocating for gender equality is a critical imperative in today's world, calling for concerted efforts to dismantle systemic barriers, biases, and inequalities that hinder the advancement of women and marginalized genders. By advocating for gender equality, individuals and organizations strive to create a more just, inclusive, and equitable society where everyone has equal opportunities to thrive and succeed, regardless of gender identity or expression. Through education, awareness-raising, policy advocacy, and collective action, advocates work to address gender-based discrimination, promote diversity and representation, and empower women and girls to realize their full potential and contribute their talents to the world. Advocating for gender equality is not only a moral imperative but also a strategic imperative for building stronger, more resilient communities and unlocking the untapped potential of half the population.

Taking Action to Promote Diversity and Inclusion

Advocating for gender equality and taking action to promote diversity and inclusion are critical steps towards creating more equitable and inclusive workplaces and societies. Here are some strategies to effectively advocate for gender equality and promote diversity and inclusion:

Educate Yourself: Start by educating yourself about gender equality issues, including the root causes of gender discrimination, disparities in representation and opportunity, and the importance of diversity and inclusion in driving innovation and success. Stay informed about current events, research, and best practices related to gender equality and diversity.

Raise Awareness: Use your voice and platform to raise awareness about gender equality and diversity issues within your organization, community, and society at large. Start conversations, share information and resources, and challenge stereotypes and biases that perpetuate inequality and discrimination.

Lead by Example: Lead by example by demonstrating inclusive behaviours and advocating for gender equality and diversity in your interactions, decisions, and actions. Be intentional about creating opportunities for diverse voices to be heard and valued, and model inclusive leadership practices for others to emulate.

Support Policy and Systemic Change: Advocate for policy and systemic changes that promote gender equality and diversity in the workplace, education, government, and society. Support legislation and initiatives that address gender-based discrimination, pay equity, parental leave, childcare access, and other systemic barriers to gender equality.

Promote Representation and Visibility: Advocate for greater representation and visibility of women and underrepresented groups in leadership positions, decision-making roles, and public forums. Support initiatives to increase diversity on boards of directors, in executive leadership teams, and in media and entertainment.

Create Inclusive Work Environments: Advocate for the creation of inclusive work environments where all employees feel valued, respected, and empowered to contribute their unique perspectives and talents. Support initiatives such as employee resource groups, diversity training, mentorship programs, and flexible work arrangements that promote inclusivity and belonging.

Address Bias and Discrimination: Take action to address bias and discrimination in hiring, promotion, and performance evaluation processes. Advocate for unconscious bias training for employees and leaders, implement blind recruitment practices, and establish clear policies and procedures to prevent and address discrimination and harassment.

Support Women and Underrepresented Groups: Support women and underrepresented groups in their professional development and advancement by providing mentorship, sponsorship, and networking opportunities. Advocate for equal access to resources, opportunities, and support systems that enable individuals from diverse backgrounds to thrive and succeed.

Collaborate and Allyship: Collaborate with others who share your commitment to gender equality and diversity, including colleagues, organizations, and community groups. Build alliances and coalitions to amplify your impact and advocate for change on a broader scale. Practice allyship by actively supporting and advocating for marginalized individuals and communities.

Measure and Evaluate Progress: Monitor progress and outcomes related to gender equality and diversity initiatives, and hold yourself and others accountable for driving meaningful change. Collect data, track metrics, and evaluate the impact of advocacy efforts to ensure that they are making a measurable difference.

By advocating for gender equality and promoting diversity and inclusion, you can contribute to creating more equitable, inclusive, and prosperous organizations and societies where everyone has the opportunity to thrive and succeed, regardless of gender, race, ethnicity, or other identities.

Supporting Other Women in Their Career Journeys

Supporting other women in their career journeys is essential for fostering a culture of solidarity, empowerment, and collective success. Here are some ways to effectively support and empower women in their careers:

Provide Mentorship: Offer mentorship to women at various stages of their careers by sharing your knowledge, expertise, and insights. Serve as a role model and sounding board, offering guidance, advice, and encouragement to help them navigate challenges, set goals, and achieve their aspirations.

Offer Sponsorship: Act as a sponsor for women by advocating for their advancement and visibility within your organization or industry.

Use your influence and networks to connect them with opportunities, projects, and influential stakeholders that can help accelerate their career growth and progression.

Create Networking Opportunities: Facilitate networking opportunities for women to connect with peers, mentors, and potential collaborators within their field. Organize networking events, workshops, or virtual forums where women can share experiences, exchange ideas, and build supportive professional relationships.

Celebrate Achievements: Celebrate the achievements and successes of women in your workplace or community by acknowledging their contributions and highlighting their accomplishments. Recognize their efforts publicly through awards, accolades, or social media shout-outs to boost their confidence and visibility.

Provide Professional Development Resources: Share resources, tools, and opportunities for professional development with women to help them enhance their skills, expand their knowledge, and advance their careers. Recommend relevant courses, workshops, conferences, or certifications that align with their interests and goals.

Offer Flexible Support: Be flexible and accommodating in your support for women, recognizing that everyone's career journey is unique and may require different forms of assistance. Offer flexibility in scheduling meetings, providing feedback, or accommodating personal commitments to ensure women can balance work and life responsibilities effectively.

Encourage Risk-Taking and Growth: Encourage women to step out of their comfort zones, take risks, and pursue new challenges and opportunities for growth. Provide encouragement and support as they navigate unfamiliar territory, overcome obstacles, and build confidence in their abilities to succeed.

Combat Imposter Syndrome: Help women overcome imposter syndrome and self-doubt by offering reassurance, validation, and perspective on their accomplishments and capabilities. Encourage them to recognize and own their successes, skills, and expertise, and remind them that they belong in the spaces where they aspire to be.

Advocate for Inclusive Policies: Advocate for inclusive policies and practices within your organization or industry that support the advancement and retention of women. Push for policies such as pay equity, parental leave, flexible work arrangements, and mentorship programs that create a more supportive and equitable workplace for women.

Be an Active Listener and Ally: Be an active listener and ally for women by creating a safe and supportive environment where they feel heard, valued, and respected. Listen to their experiences, concerns, and aspirations without judgment, and offer empathy, validation, and encouragement as needed.

By actively supporting and empowering other women in their career journeys, you contribute to building a more inclusive, diverse, and equitable workforce where all individuals have the opportunity to thrive and succeed. Your support can make a significant difference in helping women overcome barriers, achieve their goals, and reach their full potential in their careers and beyond.

Chapter 12: Breaking Barriers and Shattering Glass Ceilings

Breaking barriers and shattering glass ceilings is a courageous and transformative endeavour that entails challenging entrenched norms, biases, and limitations that obstruct the progress of underrepresented individuals, particularly women, in various spheres of life. By breaking barriers, individuals defy societal expectations, push past obstacles, and pave the way for greater inclusivity, diversity, and opportunity. Shattering glass ceilings symbolizes the triumph of resilience, determination, and merit over systemic discrimination and inequality, inspiring future generations to dream big, aim high, and pursue their aspirations without constraint. Through collective advocacy, mentorship, and allyship, individuals and communities can dismantle barriers, create pathways to success, and foster environments where everyone has the chance to rise to their full potential, irrespective of gender, race, or background.

Paving the Way for Future Generations of Female Leaders

Paving the way for future generations of female leaders is a noble and impactful endeavour that involves creating opportunities, breaking down barriers, and fostering a culture of empowerment and inclusion. Here are some key strategies to pave the way for future female leaders:

Lead by Example: Lead by example by demonstrating inclusive leadership behaviours and embodying the qualities and values you want to see in future leaders. Serve as a role model and inspiration for others by showcasing resilience, integrity, and compassion in your leadership approach.

Advocate for Change: Advocate for systemic change and policy reforms that promote gender equity and inclusion in leadership positions. Support initiatives to address gender-based discrimination, close the gender pay gap, and increase representation of women in decision-making roles across industries and sectors.

Provide Mentorship and Sponsorship: Mentor and sponsor aspiring female leaders by offering guidance, support, and opportunities for growth and advancement. Share your experiences, insights, and lessons learned to help them navigate their career paths and overcome obstacles along the way.

Create Pathways to Leadership: Create pathways to leadership by identifying and developing emerging female talent within your organization or community. Provide access to leadership development programs, training, and networking opportunities to help women build the skills and confidence needed to assume leadership roles.

Promote Diversity and Inclusion: Promote diversity and inclusion in leadership by actively seeking out and advocating for women from diverse backgrounds and experiences. Foster a culture of belonging where all individuals feel valued, respected, and empowered to contribute their unique perspectives and talents.

Challenge Stereotypes and Bias: Challenge stereotypes and bias that perpetuate gender inequality and limit opportunities for women in leadership. Raise awareness about unconscious bias, microaggressions, and systemic barriers that disproportionately affect women, and work to dismantle these barriers through education, advocacy, and allyship.

Encourage Risk-Taking and Resilience: Encourage women to take risks, pursue ambitious goals, and embrace failure as a learning opportunity on their leadership journey. Foster a culture of resilience and perseverance where setbacks are viewed as temporary setbacks rather than permanent barriers to success.

Create Supportive Networks: Create supportive networks and communities where women can connect, collaborate, and uplift each other as they navigate their leadership paths. Establish mentorship programs, affinity groups, and peer support networks to provide encouragement, advice, and solidarity to aspiring female leaders.

Amplify Women's Voices: Amplify women's voices and contributions by providing platforms and opportunities for them to share their expertise, insights, and perspectives. Ensure that women are represented and heard in decision-making processes, public forums, and media channels to help elevate their visibility and influence.

Celebrate Successes and Milestones: Celebrate the successes and milestones of female leaders and trailblazers, both within your organization and in the broader community. Recognize their achievements publicly and highlight their contributions to inspire and motivate future generations of female leaders.

By actively paving the way for future generations of female leaders, you contribute to creating a more equitable, inclusive, and diverse world where women have equal opportunities to lead, succeed, and make a positive impact on society. Your efforts today will help shape a brighter future for generations of female leaders to come.

Leaving Your Mark on the World as a Girl-Boss

Leaving your mark on the world as a Girl-Boss is about more than just achieving success in your career; it's about making a lasting impact, creating positive change, and empowering others to do the same. Here are some ways to leave your mark on the world as a Girl-Boss:

Define Your Purpose: Clarify your purpose and vision for how you want to make a difference in the world. What are your passions, values, and goals? How do you want to use your skills and talents to create positive change? Define your purpose and let it guide your actions and decisions as a leader.

Lead with Integrity: Lead with integrity, authenticity, and transparency in everything you do. Demonstrate honesty, fairness, and ethical behaviour in your interactions with others, and uphold your values and principles, even in the face of challenges or adversity.

Champion Diversity and Inclusion: Champion diversity and inclusion in your workplace, industry, and community. Create opportunities for women and underrepresented groups to thrive and succeed, and advocate for policies and practices that promote equity, fairness, and belonging for all.

Empower Others: Empower others to reach their full potential by providing mentorship, support, and opportunities for growth and development. Create a culture of empowerment where everyone feels valued, respected, and empowered to make a difference.

Be a Trailblazer: Be a trailblazer and pave the way for other women to follow in your footsteps. Break down barriers, challenge stereotypes, and defy expectations by pursuing your goals with passion, determination, and resilience.

Pay It Forward: Pay it forward by investing in the next generation of female leaders and entrepreneurs. Share your knowledge, experiences, and resources with others, and provide mentorship and support to help them succeed.

Create Positive Change: Use your influence and platform to create positive change in your community and beyond. Get involved in causes and initiatives that align with your values and passions, and leverage your skills and resources to make a meaningful impact.

Lead with Heart: Lead with heart and compassion, and prioritize the well-being and success of those around you. Listen to others with empathy and understanding, and strive to create a supportive and nurturing environment where everyone can thrive.

Leave a Legacy: Leave a legacy that inspires and empowers others to continue the work of creating positive change. Whether it's through your achievements, contributions, or the lives you touch along the way, strive to leave a lasting impact that will be remembered for generations to come.

Stay True to Yourself: Above all, stay true to yourself and your values as you strive to leave your mark on the world. Embrace your uniqueness, embrace your voice, and embrace your power as a Girl-Boss to make a difference and leave the world a better place than you found it.

Chapter 13: Conclusion

Embracing Your Power and Potential as a Girl-Boss

Embracing your power and potential as a Girl-Boss is about recognizing and owning your unique strengths, talents, and abilities as a leader. It's about stepping into your authenticity, embracing your voice, and confidently pursuing your goals and ambitions. Here are some key ways to embrace your power and potential as a Girl-Boss:

Know Your Worth: Recognize your inherent value and worth as a leader, and believe in yourself and your abilities. Celebrate your accomplishments, skills, and strengths, and don't be afraid to own your successes and achievements.

Trust Your Instincts: Trust your instincts and intuition as a leader, and have confidence in your judgment and decision-making abilities. Listen to your inner voice, follow your passion, and trust that you have the wisdom and insight to navigate challenges and seize opportunities.

Set Bold Goals: Set bold and ambitious goals for yourself and your business, and don't be afraid to dream big. Set clear intentions, create a vision for success, and take proactive steps to turn your goals into reality.

Take Action: Take decisive action towards your goals and aspirations, and don't let fear or self-doubt hold you back. Embrace a mindset of courage and resilience, and be willing to step outside of your comfort zone in pursuit of your dreams.

Build Your Confidence: Cultivate confidence in yourself and your abilities through positive self-talk, self-care, and self-affirmation. Surround yourself with supportive people who believe in you and uplift you, and let go of negative self-limiting beliefs that hold you back.

Embrace Failure as Growth: Embrace failure as a natural part of the learning and growth process, and see setbacks as opportunities for resilience and self-discovery. Learn from your mistakes, adapt to challenges, and use adversity as fuel to propel you forward.

Seek Feedback and Support: Seek feedback and support from mentors, colleagues, and peers who can offer guidance, advice, and perspective on your journey as a leader. Be open to constructive criticism and continuous improvement, and use feedback as a tool for personal and professional growth.

Lead with Authenticity: Lead with authenticity and integrity, and stay true to your values, principles, and purpose as a leader. Be genuine, transparent, and honest in your interactions with others, and build trust and credibility through your actions and words.

Celebrate Your Successes: Celebrate your successes and milestones along the way, no matter how small or seemingly insignificant. Take time to acknowledge and appreciate your achievements, and use them as motivation to keep pushing forward towards your goals.

Inspire Others: Inspire and empower others to embrace their power and potential as leaders by sharing your journey, insights, and lessons learned. Lead by example, mentor others, and create opportunities for others to shine and succeed alongside you.

By embracing your power and potential as a Girl-Boss, you can unleash your full potential as a leader, inspire others, and make a meaningful impact in your business, community, and beyond. Remember that your unique perspective, voice, and leadership style have the power to change the world for the better.

Committing to Continued Growth and Leadership

Committing to continued growth and leadership is a lifelong journey of self-discovery, learning, and development. It requires a mindset of curiosity, resilience, and continuous improvement, as well as a dedication to honing your skills, expanding your knowledge, and evolving as a leader. Here are some key ways to commit to continued growth and leadership:

Embrace a Growth Mindset: Embrace a growth mindset by believing in your capacity to learn, adapt, and grow throughout your life and career. Embrace challenges as opportunities for growth, view failure as a stepping stone to success, and cultivate a positive attitude towards learning and development.

Set Learning Goals: Set specific learning goals for yourself that align with your personal and professional aspirations. Identify areas for growth and development, whether it's acquiring new skills, expanding your knowledge base, or developing your leadership capabilities, and create a plan to achieve your goals.

Invest in Education and Training: Invest in your education and professional development by seeking out opportunities for formal education, training programs, workshops, and seminars. Stay informed about emerging trends, best practices, and industry developments relevant to your field, and seek out opportunities to deepen your expertise and skills.

Seek Feedback and Reflection: Seek feedback from mentors, colleagues, and peers to gain insights into your strengths, areas for improvement, and leadership style. Reflect on your experiences, successes, and setbacks, and use feedback as a tool for growth and self-awareness.

Challenge Yourself: Challenge yourself to step outside of your comfort zone and take on new opportunities and responsibilities that stretch your skills and abilities. Volunteer for leadership roles, projects, or initiatives that push you to grow and develop as a leader, and don't be afraid to take calculated risks.

Cultivate Self-Reflection: Cultivate a habit of self-reflection by regularly taking time to assess your progress, goals, and priorities. Set aside time for introspection, journaling, or mindfulness practices to gain clarity and perspective on your values, aspirations, and leadership journey.

Stay Curious and Open-Minded: Stay curious and open-minded by seeking out diverse perspectives, experiences, and ideas that challenge your assumptions and broaden your worldview. Stay informed about current events, research, and thought leadership in your field, and engage in conversations with others who have different backgrounds and viewpoints.

Lead by Example: Lead by example by demonstrating a commitment to growth and leadership in your actions and behaviours. Be a role model for others by embodying the qualities of a lifelong learner, taking ownership of your development, and inspiring those around you to do the same.

Build a Support Network: Build a support network of mentors, advisors, and peers who can offer guidance, support, and encouragement on your journey of growth and leadership. Surround yourself with people who believe in your potential and challenge you to be your best self.

Stay Resilient and Persistent: Stay resilient and persistent in the face of challenges, setbacks, and obstacles that may arise along your leadership journey. Approach challenges as opportunities for growth and learning, and persevere with determination and optimism, knowing that each experience brings valuable lessons and insights.

By committing to continued growth and leadership, you can unlock your full potential, expand your impact, and make a meaningful difference in your life, your organization, and the world around you. Remember that leadership is not a destination but a journey, and the path to greatness is paved with dedication, perseverance, and a relentless pursuit of excellence.

Chapter 14: Additional Resources

Books, Podcasts, and Websites on Women in Leadership

Books:

"Lean In: Women, Work, and the Will to Lead" by Sheryl Sandberg - This book offers insights and advice on navigating the challenges women face in the workplace and achieving leadership positions.

"Becoming" by Michelle Obama - Michelle Obama shares her personal journey and lessons learned as a woman in leadership, offering inspiration and empowerment to readers.

"Dare to Lead: Brave Work. Tough Conversations. Whole Hearts." by Brené Brown

- Brené Brown explores the qualities of effective leadership, including vulnerability, courage, and empathy, with practical strategies for aspiring leaders.

"The Confidence Code: The Science and Art of Self-Assurance—What Women Should Know" by Katty Kay and Claire Shipman - This book explores the factors that contribute to confidence and offers strategies for women to build confidence and assertiveness in their professional lives.

"Nice Girls Don't Get the Corner Office: Unconscious Mistakes Women Make That Sabotage Their Careers" by Lois P. Frankel - Lois Frankel identifies common mistakes women make in the workplace and provides practical advice for overcoming barriers to career advancement.

Podcasts:

"Women at Work" by Harvard Business Review - This podcast explores topics related to women in the workplace, including leadership, gender bias, and work-life balance, with insights from experts and real-world experiences.

"The Broad Experience" by Ashley Milne-Tyte - This podcast examines issues facing women in the workplace, such as gender discrimination, imposter syndrome, and negotiating salary, through interviews and discussions with thought leaders and professionals.

"Women Rule" by POLITICO - This podcast features conversations with women leaders in politics, business, and advocacy, offering insights into their experiences and perspectives on leadership and gender equality.

"Women's Leadership Success" by Sabrina Braham - This podcast provides practical tips and strategies for women to develop their leadership skills, overcome challenges, and achieve success in their careers.

"The Femails" by Career Contessa - This podcast covers a range of topics related to women in the workplace, including negotiation, personal branding, and navigating career transitions, with advice from experts and real-world stories.

Websites:

Catalyst (catalyst.org) - Catalyst is a global nonprofit organization focused on advancing women in the workplace, offering research, resources, and solutions to promote gender equality and inclusive leadership.

Lean In (leanin.org) - Lean In, founded by Sheryl Sandberg, offers resources and community support for women to achieve their ambitions and overcome gender barriers in the workplace.

Women in Leadership (womeninleadership.ie) - Women in Leadership is an initiative in Ireland that promotes gender diversity in leadership roles through research, events, and advocacy efforts.

The Female Lead (thefemalelead.com) - The Female Lead is a nonprofit organization dedicated to showcasing inspiring female role models and empowering the next generation of women leaders through education and storytelling.

Forbes Women (forbes.com/women) - Forbes Women features articles, interviews, and profiles of women leaders and entrepreneurs, providing insights and inspiration for women seeking to advance in their careers and industries.

Organizations and Networks for Female Professionals

There are several online organizations and networks specifically designed to support and connect female professionals. Here are some notable ones:

Ellevate Network (ellevatenetwork.com): Ellevate Network is a global community of professional women committed to supporting each other's career success. They offer networking events, webinars, mentorship programs, and resources to help women advance in their careers.

Lean In Circles (leanin.org/circles): Lean In Circles are small groups of women who come together regularly to support each other's personal and professional growth. These circles provide a safe space for women to share experiences, offer advice, and inspire one another to achieve their goals.

Women in Technology International (WITI) (witi.com): WITI is a leading global organization dedicated to empowering women in science, technology, engineering, and math (STEM) fields. They offer networking events, webinars, career coaching, and resources to help women thrive in the tech industry.

National Association of Women Business Owners (NAWBO) (nawbo.org): NAWBO is a membership-based organization that supports women entrepreneurs and business owners. They offer networking opportunities, educational programs, advocacy efforts, and resources to help women succeed in business.

Women's Business Enterprise National Council (WBENC) (wbenc.org): WBENC is the largest certifier of women-owned businesses in the United States. They provide networking events, educational programs, business development opportunities, and certification services to support women-owned businesses and promote supplier diversity.

Forte Foundation (fortefoundation.org): Forte Foundation is a nonprofit organization dedicated to empowering women to achieve career success through education, networking, and professional development opportunities. They offer programs for women pursuing MBA degrees and careers in business.

Women in Finance Network (womeninfinancenetwork.com): Women in Finance Network is a global community of female professionals in the finance industry. They offer networking events, mentorship programs, educational resources, and career development opportunities to support women in finance.

National Association of Professional Women (NAPW) (napw.com): NAPW is a networking organization for professional women across various industries. They offer networking events, educational webinars, career coaching, and resources to help women advance in their careers and achieve their goals.

Women in Healthcare (womeninhealthcare.org): Women in Healthcare is a professional network for women working in the healthcare industry. They provide networking opportunities, leadership development programs, mentorship initiatives, and resources to support women's career advancement in healthcare.

Women in Leadership Institute (womeninleadershipinstitute.com): The Women in Leadership Institute offers leadership development programs, conferences, and resources to help women advance into leadership roles across different sectors and industries. They focus on building leadership skills, fostering mentorship relationships, and promoting gender diversity in leadership.

Disclaimer: The information provided in this eBook is for educational and informational purposes only and is not intended as a substitute for professional advice or guidance. Readers are encouraged to seek support from qualified professionals as needed.

www.ingramcontent.com/pod-product-compliance
Lightning Source LLC
Chambersburg PA
CBHW031423210526
45464CB00005B/2031